MIND VS. MUSCLE

THE PSYCHOLOGY OF SPORTS

FOOTBALL

CATHLEEN SMALL

Gareth Stevens PUBLISHING

Please visit our website, **www.garethstevens.com**.
For a free color catalog of all our high-quality books,
call toll free 1-800-542-2595 or fax 1-877-542-2596.

Cataloging-in-Publication Data

Names: Small, Cathleen.
Title: Football / Cathleen Small.
Description: New York : Gareth Stevens Publishing, 2019. | Series: Mind vs muscle: the psychology of sports | Includes glossary and index.
Identifiers: LCCN ISBN 9781538225356 (pbk.) | ISBN 9781538225400 (library bound)
Subjects: LCSH: Football--Juvenile literature.
Classification: LCC GV950.7 S63 2019 | DDC 796.332--dc23

First Edition

Published in 2019 by
Gareth Stevens Publishing
111 East 14th Street, Suite 349
New York, NY 10003

Produced for Gareth Stevens by Calcium Creative Ltd
Editors: Sarah Eason and Jennifer Sanderson
Designers: Paul Myerscough and Simon Borrough
Picture researcher: Rachel Blount

Picture credits: Cover: Shutterstock: Aspen Photo; Inside: Shutterstock: Aspen Photo: pp. 1, 15, 25, 27, 29, 30, 36, 38, 43; Brocreative: p. 40; Ken Durden: p. 32; Eric Broder Van Dyke: p. 22; Enterlinedesign: p. 12; Mark Herreid: p. 21; Richard Paul Kane: p. 26; Margaret Kite: p. 16; John J. Klaiber Jr: p. 34; Herbert Kratky: pp. 4, 45; Kurtjurgen: p. 11; David Lee: p. 20; Lightspring: p. 5; Loongstyle: p. 24; Master1305: p. 42; Mtsaride: p. 14; Sergey Nivens: p. 39; Eugene Onischenko: p. 44; Daniel Padavona: p. 31; G Allen Penton: p. 6; Andy Pressman: p. 8; Ivelin Radkov: p. 23; Jerry Sharp: p. 13; Sirtravelalot: pp. 10, 18; Joseph Sohm: p. 19; Alexey Stiop: p. 7; StudioOneNine: p. 17; Suzanne Tucker: p. 41; Debby Wong: p. 9; Wikimedia Commons: p. 28; Keith Allison: p. 37; Jeffrey Beall: p. 33.

Printed in the United States of America

CPSIA compliance information: Batch #CS18GS.
For further information contact Gareth Stevens, New York, New York, at 1-800-542-2595.

CONTENTS

CHAPTER 1

THE PSYCHOLOGY OF Sports

Most sports are a combination of **athleticism** and mental strategy. Players need to have the physical ability to perform well, so that they can play the sport. However, they also need to understand the strategies of the sport. And they need to apply psychology to use those strategies to win the game.

Athleticism is key for a player to find success in professional football, but it is not the only ingredient of success.

UNDERSTANDING PSYCHOLOGY

Psychology can help people in any area of life. People visit psychologists to learn how to deal with difficult situations in their lives, such as divorces or separations, job losses, or deaths. Psychologists are there to listen, but also to teach people strategies for how to cope with challenging circumstances and how to maintain a healthy emotional balance in their lives.

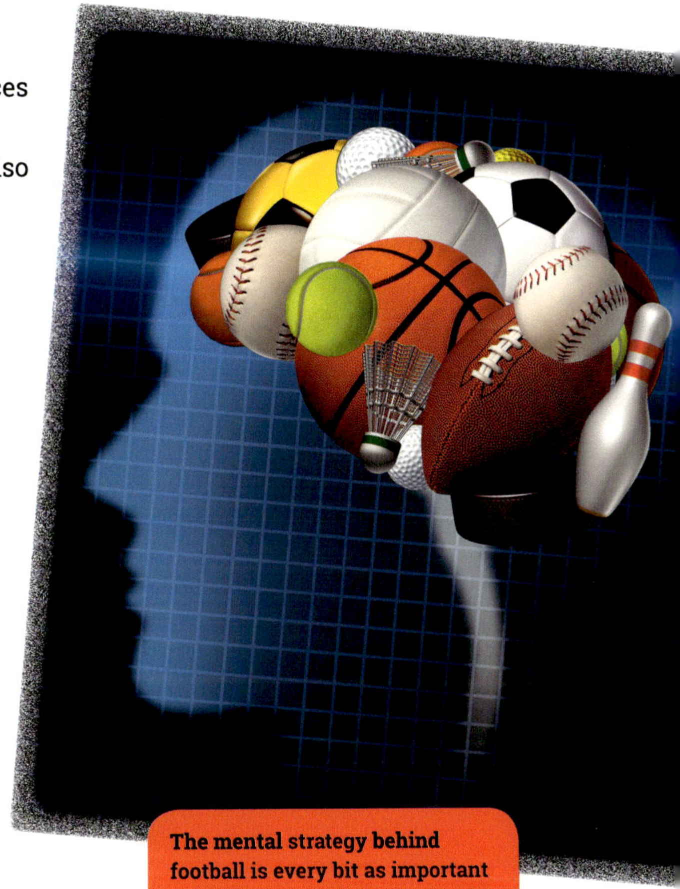

The mental strategy behind football is every bit as important as athleticism. Players work with sports psychologists to remain mentally strong and game ready.

Some psychologists encourage **meditation** to help their patients relax and focus, which helps them keep balance in their lives. Others teach their patients to write down their emotions, so they have a safe outlet for their frustration. They may also teach coping techniques for situations that bring about anxiety, such as public speaking or interviewing for a new job.

There is really no limit to what psychologists can help people with. Sports is just one of the many areas in which people benefit from working with psychologists.

WHAT IS SPORTS PSYCHOLOGY?

Sports psychology may sound like something new, but it has been in existence since the late 1800s, when Norman Triplett performed studies on the psychology behind competitive cycling. In 1925, the University of Illinois opened the first U.S. sports psychology laboratory. In that same time frame, psychologists from Stanford University in California worked in the field of football psychology.

Sports psychologists work with individual players and coaches, as well as with whole teams. Players use sports psychology techniques to enhance their performance. Coaches use these same techniques to maximize their team's potential. Some of the techniques psychologists use with athletes include **visualization**, **self-talk**, and **goal setting**. When used together, these techniques can greatly improve an athlete's game.

Mental strategy is an essential part of achieving in sports. This is particularly true in football, a game of many different, complicated strategies.

MIND VS. MUSCLE

ALL DOWN TO PERSONALITY

People cannot change their personality, but they can use their personality to make them even stronger in a particular position. Football coaches have found that certain positions tend to attract players with certain personalities.

For example, quarterbacks are the leaders—the offensive players who get the most attention. Jim Lippincott, director of football operations for the Cincinnati Bengals, describes the quarterback as the face of the team. He says that quarterbacks have to act like **CEOs** and **dominate** a field. Quarterbacks must have leadership skills, which Lippincott believes can also be taught. If quarterbacks have the raw material, they can be taught the leadership skills to make them great team leaders.

Great football players have self-belief and an inner "voice" that tells them they can succeed.

Sports psychologists can help both individual players and teams find success on the football field.

PSYCHOLOGY IN FOOTBALL

At a basic level, football players and coaches use psychology to sum up the opposing team and plan their strategy. Perhaps an opposing team has one star player, but the rest of the team is fairly average. In such a case, the team might increase its defensive coverage of the star player. The team might also build up its offense when the star player is off the field. This is mental strategy at its simplest.

On a more complex level, sports psychologists help football players use techniques such as goal setting, visualization, self-talk, and **preperformance routines**. These are all useful strategies that can improve a player's performance on the field.

Football players must learn to get in the right mind-set before stepping onto the field for a big game.

BASIC TECHNIQUES

Players can set goals to focus on improving problem areas. Sports psychologists generally recommend that players set simple, achievable goals, rather than larger, long-term goals. Long-term goals have their place, but they can be disheartening if they are too difficult to reach or too far in the future—there is no thrill of achievement if a goal is so far out of reach that it is unlikely to happen. The thrill of achievement is part of what keeps a player motivated. So, while a college football player may dream of someday winning a **Heisman Trophy**, a sports psychologist would be likely to encourage the player to also set some smaller, more manageable goals to work toward. Each smaller goal would be a step toward that Heisman Trophy.

To boost confidence and performance, players can combine goal setting with visualizing themselves performing the activity to the level they want. There is a saying "seeing is believing," and this is the idea that visualization builds upon. If players see themselves playing at a high level, eventually, they will start to believe that they can play that way. That belief will mean better play on the field.

Self-talk cues can remind players to focus on one technique. If a player tries to focus on too many things at once, it becomes difficult to focus on the game as a whole. So, sports psychologists may give players some self-talk cues to remind them of what they should be focusing on.

Preperformance routines can build up the player's **muscle memory** to improve performance during the game. Games are fast-paced, and players often do not have time to think about their actions. They need to move on instinct. Coaches and sports psychologists help players learn to move on instinct by creating preperformance routines that become so ingrained in the players, that their muscle memory takes over during the game.

These are just a few of the many ways sports psychologists can help football players and coaches. When psychological strategies are used along with mental strategies to map out the plays, players can really improve. Psychological game plans give players a confidence and performance boost, and the mental strategies can help players outsmart the opposing team.

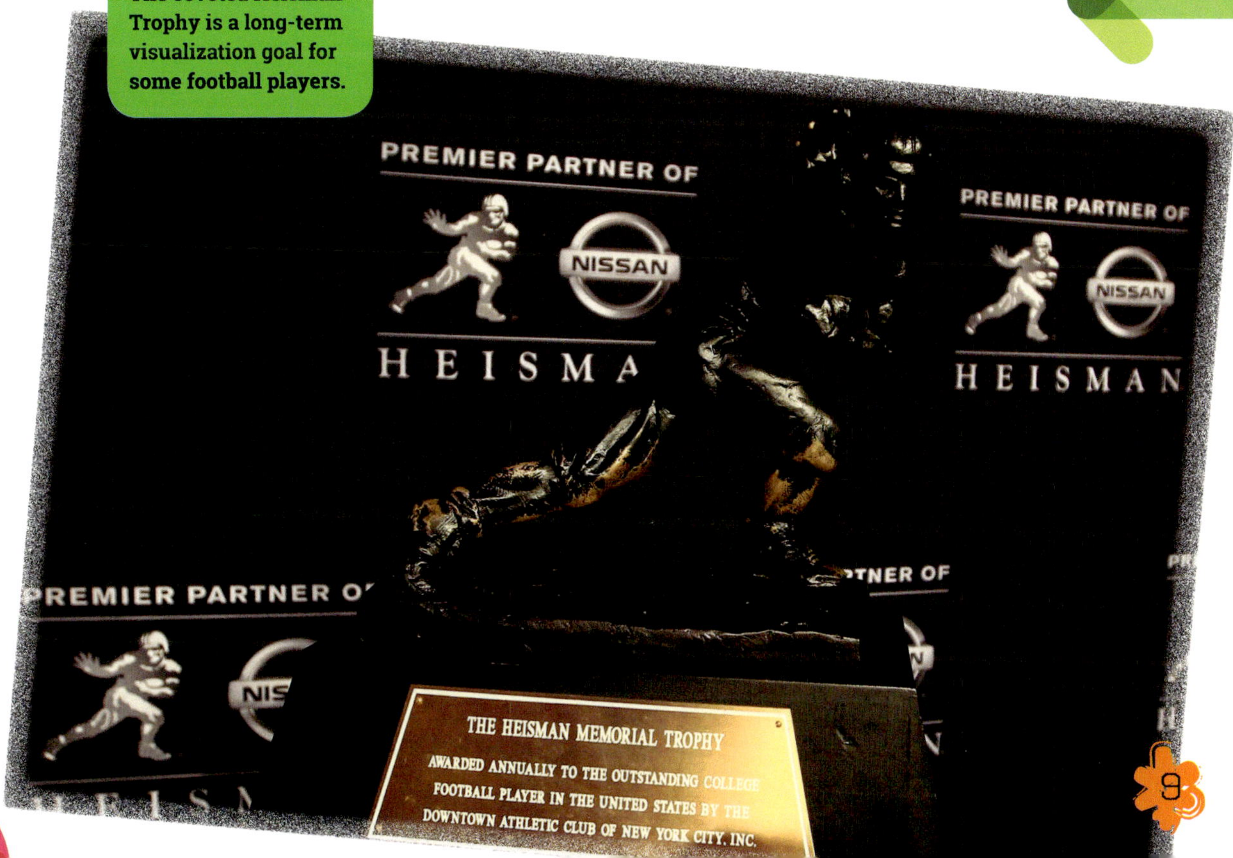

The coveted Heisman Trophy is a long-term visualization goal for some football players.

CHAPTER 2

THE BASICS OF Football

Football in the United States began in 1869. However, it did not become really popular until the late 1950s and early 1960s. As long as the game has existed, players and coaches have used strategy and psychology to improve their teams' play. The use of strategy skyrocketed along with the game's popularity in the 1950s and 1960s. It was then that football became the game that people know and love today.

Spectators love to sit and watch football games, acting as **armchair quarterbacks** and analyzing the strategy and athletic play. Football is appealing because it combines things sports fans enjoy: brute strength and athleticism with strategy.

Football is incredibly popular among many Americans. A pickup game can often take place at family gatherings.

Football fields may or may not be enclosed in stadiums. Any field will do for a pickup game of football.

THE LOCATION

Football is played on a field, and technically, it can be played on any field. Pickup football games are popular at social gatherings, such as outdoor family events and picnics. When families gather together to celebrate holidays such as Thanksgiving, it is not unusual for a pickup football game to break out. All people need is an open space, something to designate the goal line, and a ball.

Pickup football games can—and have—also been played in the street. However, football involves tackling, which could be quite painful on asphalt. So, people playing football on anything other than a field often opt to play flag football. In this game, players remove a flag from an opponent's waistband instead of tackling them.

In competitive football, games are played on a rectangular field that is 120 yards (110 m) long. The field is 53.33 yards (49 m) wide. At each end of the field is a line called the end line. Running up each side of the field, between the end lines, are the sidelines, and 10 yards (9 m) in from each end line is a goal line.

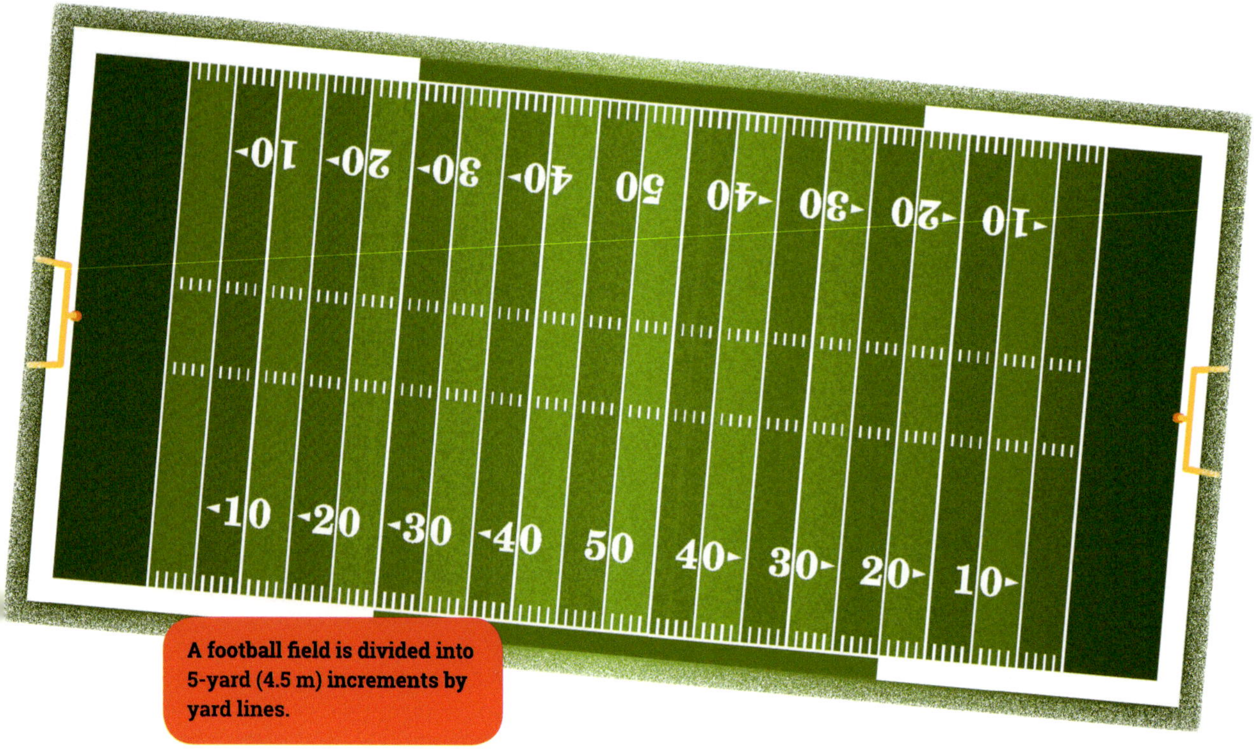

A football field is divided into 5-yard (4.5 m) increments by yard lines.

The field is marked by yard lines, which are marked in white every 5 yards (4.5 m). These lines identify the distance from the end zone. Between yard lines are hash marks (short parallel lines) that break down the field into 1 yard (0.9 m) sections. Each yard line that is a multiple of ten is marked by a numeral showing the number of yards from the closest goal.

At each end line, there is a goalpost. The post has a vertical bar rising from the center of the line to 10 feet (3 m) above the ground. At 10 feet (3 m), there is a horizontal crossbar on top of the post. The length of this crossbar depends on whether the goalpost is for a high school game or for a college or professional game. High school goalposts have a crossbar measuring 23.3 feet (7 m), while college and professional games have crossbars measuring 18.5 feet (6 m).

On football fields used by professional players, at each end of the crossbar are verticals upright posts that extend 35 feet (11 m). On college fields, the vertical posts extend at least 30 feet (9 m), and on high school fields, they extend at least 10 feet (3 m).

When football is played for fun or at lower levels, the field is usually grass. In professional football, the field is sometimes covered in turf.

THE TURF

Fields can be covered in grass or artificial turf. In professional football, the ratio is close to half and half, with about 50 percent of teams playing on natural grass and 50 percent playing on artificial turf.

Turf is much more durable than grass, and in some ways, it requires less maintenance: no cutting, though it does need cleaning. However, there are some safety concerns that come with using turf. Turf is harder than grass, and thus, more injuries can occur when playing on it. For example, National Football League (NFL) players are more likely to sprain the joint on their big toe when playing on turf—a condition that has come to be known as "turf toe." A study done by the NFL Injury and Safety Panel in 2012 showed that the rate of knee sprains in the NFL was 22 percent greater when players were playing on turf. Turf retains heat and can burn the skin under hot sun. It can also cause friction abrasions and burns when players slide on it during tackles.

THE EQUIPMENT

Football players do not need a lot of equipment. The goalposts are stationary on the field, so the only other thing required is the football.

Footballs are oval in shape, unlike the balls in many other sports. They weigh between 14 ounces (397 g) and 15 ounces (425 g). Professional footballs are slightly longer and wider than the balls used in high school and college games.

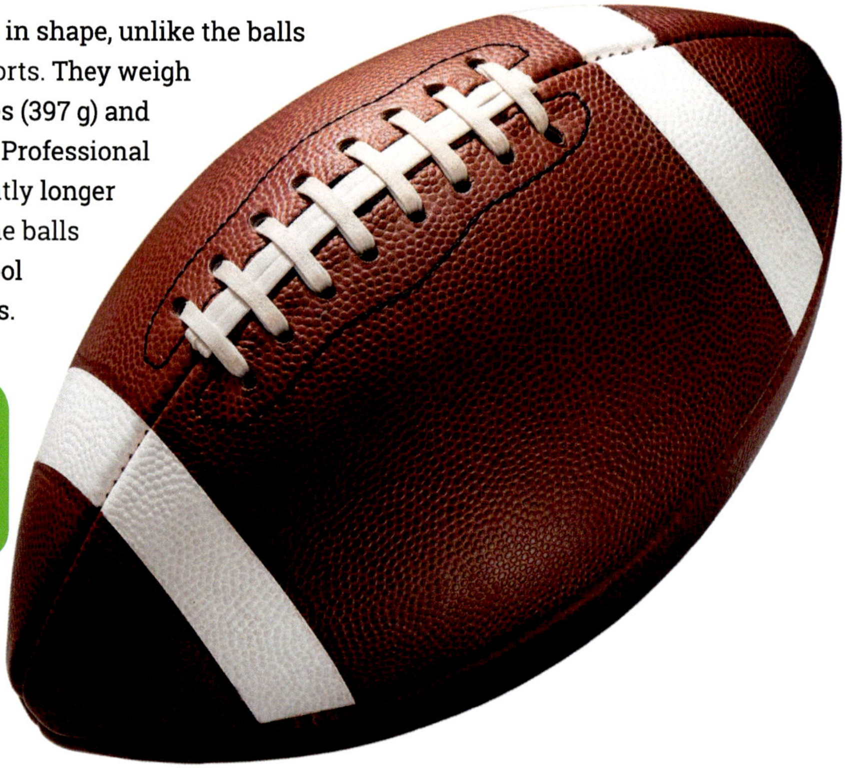

Footballs are oblong and slightly larger for professionals than for high school and college games.

THE UNIFORMS

Football uniforms consist of tight-fitting pants and a jersey. The jersey has the player's number on the front and back, and the player's last name is also often on the back above the number. In the NFL, numbers are assigned based on the player's position. For example, quarterbacks wear numbers between 1 and 19.

There is a great deal of protective gear worn, too. In football, head injuries are so common that wearing a good helmet is very important. Helmets have chinstraps to help hold them in place. Many helmets also have air-filled pockets inside them. The air provides a cushion that can help prevent head injuries, but it is also used for fit. If a helmet feels too tight, the player can release a little air from the pockets, so that the helmet fits snugly but not too tight. The helmet has metal bars on the front of it, too, which act as a kind of cage to protect the player's face.

Helmets are an essential part of a player's protective gear, but other types of padding are commonly worn, too.

Football players also **wear protective** shoulder pads, **thigh** pads, and **kneepads**. Some players also wear **elbow** pads, hip pads, and tail pads, though not all do. The shoulder pads are particularly important, because they help protect the player's collarbone, **rotator cuff**, and **sternum**, all of which are **susceptible** to injury and breakage during play.

Players wear socks and cleats, which are shoes with protrusions on the bottom, to help grip the field. Cleats come in different lengths depending on the field a player is playing on. Dry, firm fields require short cleats, whereas wet, slippery fields may require longer cleats. The shortest cleats are worn on artificial turf. However, some players prefer not to use cleats on artificial turf because they get stuck in the turf, leading to knee and ankle injuries.

Players often land in awkward positions, so helmets can help protect them from catastrophic head injuries.

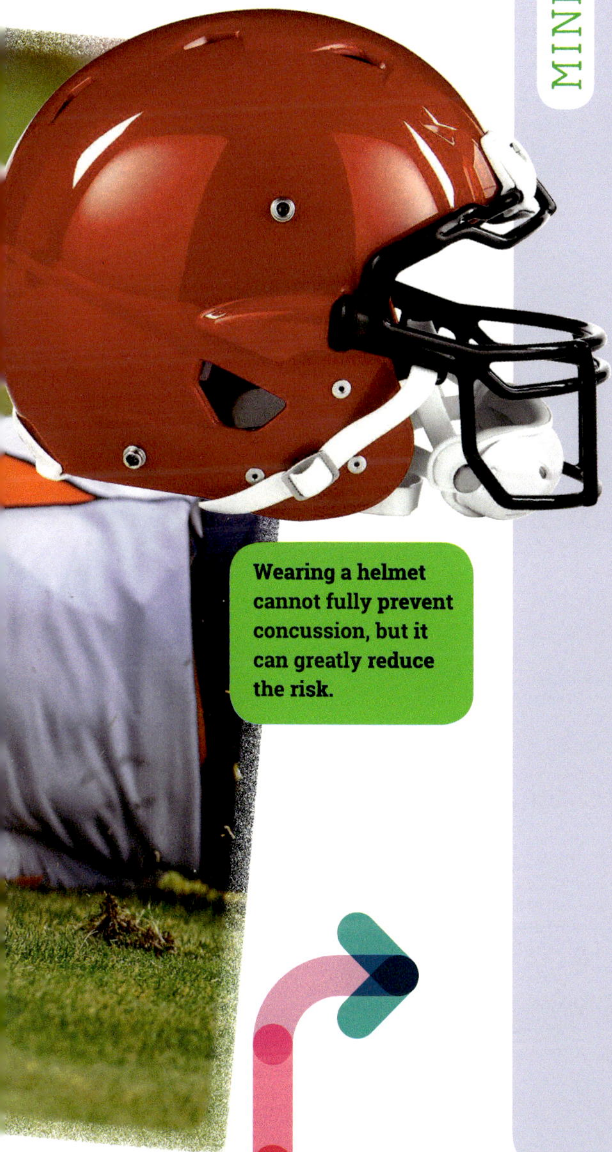

Wearing a helmet cannot fully prevent concussion, but it can greatly reduce the risk.

MIND VS. MUSCLE

PROTECTING THE BRAIN

Football is a game of athleticism and mental strategy. For the mental strategy, players need to have their brains working well. However, this is where there can be a problem: Football is a notoriously dangerous sport in terms of concussions. A concussion is a condition that occurs after a blow to the head. Sufferers may lose consciousness or feel sick or confused. Even when wearing helmets, players sometimes sustain concussions from being tackled. The medical community has given a name to the brain trauma suffered as a result of repeated blows to the head in football and other high-contact sports, such as hockey and boxing: chronic traumatic encephalopathy (CTE). It is sometimes called postconcussion **syndrome**.

In the long term, CTE has been shown to cause depression, memory loss, **dementia**, and can lead to suicide. A recent study out of Boston University, in Massachusetts, where 94 former NFL players' brains were **autopsied**, showed that 90 tested positive for CTE. Studies have shown that other neurological conditions, such as **ALS**, may also be more prevalent in football players.

There have been numerous lawsuits brought by former NFL players, alleging that the NFL knew of the dangers of CTE and neglected to address the issue. As a result of that and taking into account current information, the NFL has been actively working to reduce the number of concussions and to protect players.

CHAPTER 3

COACHING AND TEAM Strategies

In most team sports, the coach is the leader. In football, this is particularly true, because the coach generally calls the plays. The best coaches know their teams very well, and they read the team and decide the best strategy moving forward.

THE SHOTGUN STRATEGY

In 1975, Tom Landry was coaching the Dallas Cowboys, who were having a terrible season. Their previous season had been dismal, too. They had won only eight games and, for the first time in nine seasons, had not qualified for the playoffs.

The play lies in the hands of the quarterback, but usually, the coach calls the strategy.

Tom Landry, coach of the Cowboys, found great success motivating his team when he brought back a time-tested strategy: the shotgun.

Landry knew a change was needed. To try to jump-start the team, he decided to bring back an old strategy that was first used in 1960—the shotgun. The shotgun had been used by San Francisco 49ers' coach Red Hickey for just one season, and it had not been used since. The strategy works by having the quarterback stand several yards behind the center to receive the snap.

At the time, the Cowboys quarterback was Roger Staubach. He led the Cowboys to five Super Bowls and was the first player to win both the Heisman Trophy and Super Bowl **MVP**. Staubach thought Landry must have been crazy to try to use an old, almost-forgotten strategy. However, Landry knew that an unexpected "new" strategy might be just the push the team needed.

The element of surprise can be a great strategy in many ways. In the case of Landry's shotgun, it caught the opposing team off guard. They were not ready to react. Defensive back Herm Edwards, who played against the Cowboys, remembered, "It was a different look, and ... it messed up your way of looking at the quarterback's drop and defining that drop."

It also spiced up a team that had fallen into a routine of doing the same plays over and over. Football coaches look at Landry's decision as a reminder that, sometimes, the way to shake up a team stuck in a rut is by introducing something new or different. Even Staubach realized in hindsight that Landry's strategy for the team had been correct. Staubach later commented that it gave the Cowboys a real advantage, because the opposing team was not used to it and had to play against it.

BACK TO BASICS

Another coaching strategy that can be very effective is going back to basics. This is especially true when a team has been playing together for some time: Players can get into the mind-set that they know all they need to know.

Footballers spend hours practicing and perfecting tackles with equipment such as this.

MIND VS. MUSCLE

VINCE LOMBARDI: STARTING AT THE BEGINNING

When Vince Lombardi took over as coach of the Green Bay Packers in 1959, the team was in terrible shape. In fact, 1958 was the team's worst season ever—they won only one game, and they lost 10. They also tied one. Lombardi flatly told players that he had never before been part of a losing team, and he did not intend to begin then.

Instead of coming up with new strategies or replacing players with newer, fresher ones, Lombardi kept the team together. He then took them back to the very basics of football.

Lombardi knew that the older players had grown lazy in practicing the most basic skills of football. So, the smartest strategy was to make them master the fundamentals all over again.

It worked. The Packers turned around their awful record and began winning again. In the 1959 season, they won seven games and lost five. It wasn't a perfect season, but it was much better than the previous one. By 1961, the Packers were on a winning streak, finishing the season with 11 wins and only 3 losses. In 1967, under coach Lombardi, they won the Super Bowl.

Green Bay Packers quarterback Aaron Rodgers takes a snap in a game against the San Francisco 49ers.

In almost any sport, subject, or job, people sometimes need to relearn what they learned in the beginning. For example, students usually start the school year by going over what they studied the previous year. Professionals in many fields go to classes that help them relearn what they already know. This is just as true in football, when sometimes football players need to go back to basics. Coaches like Vince Lombardi recognize the importance of revisiting these skills. Lombardi used this when he took over as coach of the Green Bay Packers in 1959. Using the psychological strategy of goal setting, he made the team go through very elementary drills to remaster the basics.

Going back to basics can help even professional teams prepare to play their best on game day.

PREPLANNING THE GAME

Some coaches find it useful to create a **road map of plays** that will take place in the game. This allows the team to visualize how the game will play out when it meets its opponents. It also uses the strategy of goal setting, in that each play on the road map is a short, achievable goal to be met.

The road map can be changed, of course. If a game appears to be going in a different direction from what the coach thought it would, the plays can be changed. However, usually, having a road map for a game allows the team to rehearse how it will go.

What looks like an oddly elaborate game of tic-tac-toe is actually a coach's road map of plays.

MIND VS. MUSCLE

BILL WALSH: DRESS REHEARSAL

Bill Walsh, who coached football from 1960 to 1994, once spoke about preplanning a football game. Walsh explained that with a clear head before the game, coaches could plan out much of the game before it was even played. The coaches would review the opposing team and watch videos of past games to see the team's playing style. They would then use that information to plan out the first 20 to 25 plays of the game. This brought them almost to halftime. In the same way, they would also loosely plan the second half of the game. To build a lead, Walsh said, it was important to focus on passing in the early part of the game. Players could then run the ball against a tired defense later in the game.

CHAPTER 4

OFFENSIVE Strategies

Coaches use several strategies for both offensive and defensive plays. The strategies depend a lot on factors of a particular game. These include players on the field, plays being used by the opposing team, and weather conditions. Coaches also use strategies that involve figuring out situations as they take place and then making the best call.

OFFENSIVE SYSTEMS

Teams use two main types of offensive play: runs and passes. Runs are usually shorter plays, and passes are longer ones. Some offensive systems use a lot of runs to tire out the opposing defense. Others use a lot of passes to score as many points as they can.

Coaches and offensive coordinators call certain plays based on many factors. These might include the down, the **line of scrimmage**, and the time left in the game. Passes might work better if the team needs more yards. Runs might be best if the team is only a short distance from the end zone. The coach, or sometimes the quarterback, will figure out the situation at any given play and make the call.

Teams line up along the line of scrimmage to start the play.

Whether the play will involve a run or a pass also depends on the team's strengths, which the coach will know well. If a team has particularly strong and fast running backs, then runs may be their best strategy. The same is true if the team's offensive line dominates at the line of scrimmage and is particularly strong at run blocking, which is when an offensive lineman fires off the line of scrimmage the moment the ball is snapped. Their goal is to keep the defensive players from tackling the player who has the ball.

On the other hand, if a team's strengths lie in having strong quarterback and/or fast wide receivers, then a pass might be the better play. A strong quarterback can, in theory, gain more yards by passing the ball far down the field to the wide receivers. This strategy relies on the wide receivers being able to run faster than the defense. Once the defense realizes where the quarterback is passing the ball, the defense will run to try to intercept the pass or tackle the wide receiver when they catch the ball.

With a strong wide receiver like Jovon Durante, a pass might be the team's best offensive strategy.

Blocking is a smart offensive strategy in which the lineman blocks the opposing team, in order to create a path for their own teammate to move the ball down the field.

BLOCKING

Blocking might sound like a defensive strategy, but it is actually an offensive strategy. After the ball is snapped, the offensive team has two choices: It can pass the ball, or it can run with it. If the team decides to run, it will obviously want to gain as many yards as possible—it does not want to gain a yard or two before being tackled. That is where blocking comes in. The offensive lineman will, upon the snap, immediately push forward and block the defense, so that there is a clear path through which the team member holding the ball can run. The lineman is creating a path by blocking the defense from entering it.

This is a very important offensive job and is an offensive lineman's only job. The offensive lineman is, in fact, not allowed to catch a forward pass. They can, however, run with the ball or catch a backward pass. However, they do not do either very often, and mostly, they just focus on blocking.

FAKING

Faking is one of the oldest strategies and is used in many sports. Soccer players fake left and go right (or vice versa). Basketball players fake a pass in order to throw their opponent off guard, so they can take a shot. In some ways, the fake is the simplest of sports strategies—but also one of the most effective.

In football, a quarterback may fake to try to make the opposing team think they are going to throw a long pass, but really, they mean to throw a short pass. The team as a whole might fake a setup where it looks like the quarterback is going to run with the ball, when really, they are going to pass. There are many ways to use this simple but smart strategy in football.

A quarterback may try to fake out the opposing team as an offensive strategy.

ALL IN THE MIND

Don Hutson: The Father of Football Fakes

Don Hutson, who played for the Green Bay Packers in the 1930s and 1940s, was known for both his great catching and his speed on the field. He was also known for his smart strategy, including being the first football player to use fakes in the game.

Philadelphia Eagles coach Greasy Neale said that Hutson could **feint** in three different directions at once. In doing so, Hutson would fake out the defensive players who were trying to stall his forward movement. He could then punch a hole through the defense to make a run. At that point, his legendary speed would come in very handy.

To study the king of fakes, one need look no further than football legend Don Hutson.

SWITCH IT UP

Faking is a simple but useful offensive strategy, and along similar lines, so is switching up the plays. This strategy is very basic, and it is also used in many sports. For example, in baseball, a pitcher will mix up the pitches he throws, so that the batters on the opposing team do not start to anticipate what he will pitch.

In football, the strategy is similar. The head coach or whoever is calling the plays will mix up the plays, so that the opposing team will not be able to predict the play. A team that tends to use a lot of pass plays will face a team well prepared to intercept passes. Likewise, a team that uses a lot of running plays will face a team that has prepared to stop runs.

Many teams prepare for the game by watching recordings of their opponents' past games. They will pick up on patterns in the opposing team's play, and they will tailor their strategy accordingly. That is why one of the most important offensive strategies is to keep things unpredictable.

Head coaches have been known to switch up plays just to catch the opposing team off guard. It is a simple but effective strategy.

CHAPTER 5

DEFENSIVE Strategies

The goal of football is to score as many points as possible. The team that scores the most points wins the game. In that sense, offense is critical. Without a strong offense, the team will not be able to score points, and it will lose. However, defense is equally important, because no matter how good a team's offense is, it will lose if the opposing team is able to score points on them.

Teams use one of two main defensive systems: the 3–4 or the 4–3. The 3–4 uses three linemen and four linebackers, so it is good for stopping passes. The 4–3 uses four linemen and three linebackers, so it is better for stopping runs. The system a team uses often depends on the offensive systems used by the opposing team.

Defense is usually 4–3 or 3–4, but the goal is the same either way—to prevent the offense from moving the ball down the field.

The running back, poised to grab the ball, can be quickly brought down by a defenseman if he is well guarded.

THE 4–3 DEFENSE

Just before football became really popular in the 1950s, an important change in strategy came about. The 4–3 defense is the most popular **defensive alignment** used in modern football. It was designed to deal with an offensive strategy created by coach Paul Brown. Brown's strategy helped the offense to gain a lot of ground on the field through great passing. The strategy was so effective that defensive coaches everywhere scrambled to find a way to put a stop to it. The 4–3 was the answer.

Tom Landry was the defensive coordinator for the New York Giants between 1954 and 1959. He studied passing strategy, which was new at the time. His studies flagged an important weakness in defense strategy. When defensive players lined up along the line of scrimmage, they threw themselves into a crush of offensive players as soon as the ball was in play. Landry realized that this was relatively useless against a passing strategy.

Landry used a very simple idea to fix this problem. Players at the line of scrimmage could not see where the opposing quarterback was positioned to pass. So, if he just moved some players back from the line of scrimmage, they could better see where the opposing quarterback was planning to pass. That would allow the defensive players to figure out what the pass might be. They could then position themselves to stall the offense's forward movement.

This basic yet smart strategy has been used in football ever since, and it is one of the most-used defensive lineups. The strategy is simple, but it uses an important sports psychology technique: visualization. If the defense can see the quarterback's positioning and body language, they can visualize where the quarterback is going to pass the ball. They can then move themselves into position to stop the pass.

Cowboys coach Tom Landry moved defensive players from the line of scrimmage, so that they could see where the opposing quarterback intended to pass.

ALL IN THE MIND

Charles Woodson: Intelligent Defense

Charles Woodson, who played for the Oakland Raiders and the Green Bay Packers from 1998 to 2015, is one of the NFL's best defensive players of all time. His success on the field was incredible, given that he was born with **clubbed feet** and did not walk until the age of four.

On the field, Woodson was a great athlete. He had determination and great instinct. He also inspired his teammates. In 2004, the Oakland Raiders had won only 3 games out of 10 in the season. Then they were faced with playing the much more successful Denver Broncos in a snowstorm. The Raiders were at an obvious disadvantage. Not only were the Broncos a better team that year, but the Raiders were not used to playing in such conditions, since Oakland does not get snow. Woodson delivered a pregame speech to his teammates that inspired them so much that they went on to beat the Broncos.

Charles Woodson had some physical challenges as a child, but he more than made up for them with his intelligence on the field.

The player is poised for the play to begin at the line of scrimmage.

THE 3–4 DEFENSE

The 3–4 defense was the most commonly used defensive alignment in the late 1970s and early 1980s. It was less used in the 1990s, but in the 2000s, it began to be used more often again. Currently, it is still frequently used in the NFL.

The 3–4 defense lines up three defensive linemen (two defensive ends and one nose tackle) opposite the opposing team's offensive line. The three defensive linemen handle the offensive line for the other team, which leaves the four linebackers behind them open either to rush the quarterback or running backs, or to drop back if they expect the quarterback to pass the ball. If the linebackers expect a pass, they may cover the wide receivers, whom they expect will receive the quarterback's pass.

BLITZING

In either defensive lineup, the defense might also blitz. This is where defensive players will rush at the quarterback after the snap. Their goal is either to tackle the quarterback or pressure him into making a bad pass. They might also fake a blitz to unsettle the quarterback and push him into a hurried pass.

Blitzing can be a really effective strategy, because if the defense is able to make the quarterback nervous, he may not make a good pass. If they tackle him while he still has the ball, that is an even better outcome. However, there is risk in blitzing, too. Blitzing involves a high number of defensive players rushing the quarterback, so it leaves fewer defensive players on the back end of the field. If the quarterback manages to hand off the ball to the running back, that leaves the field more open for a long run by the running back. If the quarterback manages to pass the ball in spite of the blitz, it means the wide receivers may not be well covered by the defense, many of whom have rushed the quarterback.

The importance of strong defense cannot be stressed enough. As in offensive plays, visualization can be very helpful in defensive strategy. A team can use visualization to attempt to predict the plan of action of a quarterback, running back, or wide receivers. Then they can visualize their own attempts to stop the offense. Like most sports, football requires some level of prediction and visualization. The predictions and visualizations will not always be right, but often they will help the teams better their play on the field.

In a blitz, the defensive players rush to bring down the quarterback.

CHAPTER 6

GAME-DAY Ready!

Mental strategy is at work in all of football. Football is a complicated game in which a player must understand the psychology of the opposing team. They must also get to know the strengths and weaknesses of the individual players. Above all, the strongest mental strategy a player can use is to have an understanding of themselves.

Players need to be in peak mental shape to be ready for the big game!

All that mental strategy combined with athleticism puts a player at their strongest. When the coach encourages this approach in the whole team, it results in a winning team. An overall strategy that will improve any player's game is mental coaching. Mental coaching helps players learn how to sharpen their focus and increase their confidence. It helps them control their emotions on the field and improve their communication with their teammates. It also improves their motivation.

Sports psychology expert Dr. Jim Afremow says that mental coaching can be really useful when a player has had a setback. Setbacks might include a period of poor play, a serious injury, a losing streak, or a performance **plateau**.

Many different techniques can be used in mental coaching, including setting goals, finding **intrinsic** motivation, visualizing play, and using affirmations and positive self-talk.

ALL IN THE MIND

Tom Brady: Coaching Past a Slump

Quarterback Tom Brady has often used mental coaching to improve his performance after a slump. Although Brady is thought of as one of football's all-time greatest quarterbacks, he has had setbacks in his career. In 2016, he was suspended from four games for his part in a football-tampering scandal. He also missed 15 games in 2008 for injuries to his knee. Mental coaching helped Brady come back from both of these setbacks and pick up his strong career with the Patriots.

Mental coaching helped legendary Patriots quarterback Tom Brady move past a serious career slump.

SETTING GOALS

Goal setting is important for any athlete. Without goals, the athlete has nothing concrete to work toward. Jim Afremow states that goals can be short term or long term, but that either way, they should be clear and challenging. Short-term goals should be especially clear. A long-term goal might be a little wider, such as, "I want to play in the NFL." A short-term goal should be something very specific that the player can work toward, such as a quarterback saying, "I want to complete at least 50 percent of my long passes."

Very specific short-term goals are easy to focus on because they are so concrete: In the next game, the quarterback either achieves their 50 percent pass completion goal, or they do not. If they do not, they keep working toward it in future games. If they achieve it, perhaps they will make the goal more challenging for the next game—maybe upping the completed pass percentage to 60 percent.

A quarterback might set goals related to throwing more completed passes.

Players need to find their motivation. Is it adoration from the crowd, or is it an intrinsic desire to constantly improve their game?

It is important that short-term goals be challenging but also achievable. If players never achieve their short-term goals, it can become disheartening, which can affect their play and confidence. Achieving goals, on the other hand, is very motivating and can prompt the athlete to play even better in the next game. Reaching goals can be somewhat addictive: Players who regularly meet short-term goals are inspired to set more challenging goals and work hard to reach them.

Long-term goals are important, too, but perhaps less so than short-term goals. It is good to have a big picture to look toward, but the more concrete, achievable short-term goals are what can really motivate the player and their team.

FINDING MOTIVATION

Setting goals can also lead to finding motivation. There are two types of motivation: **extrinsic** and intrinsic. Extrinsic motivation is motivation from factors outside oneself. Examples might be fame or money. Players whose main goal is to become famous and make a lot of money are extrinsically motivated.

Intrinsic motivation is motivation that comes from inside oneself. Players who are intrinsically motivated always want to play their absolute best. They are always working to improve their skills and overall play for no other reason than they always want to be the best athlete they can.

While both intrinsic and extrinsic motivation can help inspire players, intrinsic motivation usually helps with better long-term play. If players set short-term, concrete goals for the purpose of improving their overall play, that intrinsic motivation will continue to encourage them to set new goals and always improve their game. The whole team will benefit from this.

VISUALIZING PLAY

Another mental strategy that can improve a football player's game is using visualization. Visualization is seeing in one's mind the way the players hope to play in the game.

There are two types of visualization: internal and external. In external visualization, the players "see" themselves carrying out plays in the game as if they are watching it on a movie screen. It is almost like the players are watching others playing—only in reality, they are watching themselves.

The visualization of catching a touchdown pass can help the player subconsciously feel like he has achieved this. This can then help build muscle memory.

If players are not performing well, coaches can help them visualize the play and improve their game.

Internal visualization is when players imagine their body performing the action. The players feel like they are actually enacting the plays—only they are really just imagining it. This type of visualization in particular can help build muscle memory—if the players imagine themselves carrying out plays enough times, their muscles actually start to believe they have performed the plays, which become second nature.

Both types of visualization are useful. They both help the player build confidence. If players "see" themselves playing well enough times, they begin to believe it. And it's well known that confidence improves game play for any athlete, so even confidence that comes from imagining oneself playing at the top of one's game is useful.

USING AFFIRMATIONS

Another way players can build confidence is by using affirmations and positive self-talk. Sports psychologists generally recommend daily positive affirmations. The idea is that if players hear themselves speaking positively about their abilities enough times, they will eventually believe this, and this will improve their confidence and play.

A positive affirmation for a quarterback might be something like, "I consistently throw completed passes." A positive affirmation for an offensive lineman might be something like, "When the ball is snapped, I quickly and effectively push forward to make space for the running backs to move the ball down the field."

Affirmations can be spoken or written down. For example, players who use verbal affirmations might stand in front of the mirror and recite them each morning and each evening. Or, they might recite them while on their way to a practice game.

Written affirmations can be in a journal or in a letter to oneself. Some people find writing to be a more comfortable and effective way to get the message across to themselves, while others prefer speaking. Some combine both methods: They write down positive affirmations in a journal, which they can revisit and recite to themselves.

Positive affirmations can help build winning teams.

MIND VS. MUSCLE

AFFIRMATIONS FROM THE COACH

Players can use affirmations to help build up their own confidence, but another useful strategy is for a coach to use positive affirmations with his players. Kirk Talley, the award-winning head football coach at the University of Northwestern–St. Paul in Minnesota, finds that delivering positive affirmations to players energizes them, gives them a little extra edge, and inspires them to work harder. It also sparks a new attitude and always benefits the team as a whole.

Talley says the affirmations can be as general as, "We're going to get this done!" and "We're at our best in tough situations." They can also be more targeted to a specific player, such as, "John, I believe in you." Either way, Talley says statements like these made at the right time can make a major difference to players.

Coaches can also deliver affirmations to their players to help build confidence.

Cheering fans in a stadium can be distracting, but if a player can tune them out and focus, his game will undoubtedly benefit.

FINDING FOCUS

In any sport—and football is no exception—finding focus is one of the most important mental strategies. Playing a game in front of spectators is difficult. Whether it is bleachers full of parents and fellow students, or a stadium filled with thousands of football fans, it can be very difficult for players to focus on the game when there is the distraction of cheering and booing people sitting on the sidelines.

Sports psychologists can teach players techniques to help block out the noise from the sidelines and focus on the game. Meditation is one such technique: Some players make meditation part of their pregame routine. They find a quiet place where they can be alone with their thoughts, and they meditate on being focused and free from distraction during the game. Other players find that playing a certain song or soundtrack helps get them in a focused mind-set for the game. Still others find that the very act of going through their pregame warm-up is enough to help them focus on the game.

Focus is important because football is a very fast-moving game. During the game, there is not much time to stop and think about plays—instead, players have to go with their gut and make split-second decisions. Doing so is much easier if they are in a focused mind-set and not distracted from the game.

A GAME OF WITS

On the surface, football is a game of athletic skill and raw strength. Players must be in great physical shape to run, pass, and tackle. Under the surface lies a game of complicated strategies. Players must understand the psychology of their opponents and the team as a whole. They must come to grips with the opposing team's psychology. At the same time, they must use mental strategy to improve their own play. If they can master these important mental skills, they can be part of a team that will win on the field.

Athleticism will take a player a long way in football—but mental strength will take his play to the next level.

GLOSSARY

ALS acronym for amyotrophic lateral sclerosis, which is also known as Lou Gehrig's disease. This is a degenerative disease of the nervous system, which leads to muscle deterioration and paralysis.

armchair quarterbacks people who don't play a sport but still make judgments and offer opinions about the game play

athleticism strength, fitness, and agility in an athlete

autopsied examined a dead body to find out the cause of death

CEOs acroynom for chief executive officer: the highest-ranking person at a company

clubbed feet a physical deformity in which the feet appear to be rotated in at the ankle

defensive alignment the way in which the defensive players are aligned at the start of a play

dominate exercise control over

extrinsic something that comes from outside a person

feint a quick, deceptive movement

goal setting setting small, manageable goals to achieve an overall greater goal

Heisman Trophy an award given annually to an outstanding player in college football

intrinsic something that comes from inside a person

line of scrimmage an imaginary line that separates the offense and defense at the beginning of a play

meditation a relaxation technique in which one reflects carefully on thoughts

muscle memory a form of memory in which a muscle is repeatedly trained to do a specific task

MVP acronym for most valuable player; the standout player on a team

plateau a time of no change after a period of progress

preperformance routines actions or behaviors athletes use to prepare for a game

road map of plays a general plan of the plays that a team will use in a football game

rotator cuff the muscles and tendons that surround the shoulder joint

self-talk words or phrases a person says to themselves to be more effective in reaching a goal

sternum the flat bone at the front center of the chest, to which all ribs attach. Also known as the breastbone.

visualization forming a mental image of an action or object

FOR MORE INFORMATION

BOOKS

Anastasio, Dina. *What Is the Super Bowl?* New York, NY: Grosset & Dunlap, 2015.

Doeden, Matt. *The World's Greatest Football Players.* Mankato, MN: Capstone Press, 2010.

Savage, Jeff. *Tom Brady.* Minneapolis, MN: Lerner Publications, 2015.

WEBSITES

Find out more about being healthy and keeping fit through sports at:
www.brainpop.com/health/sportsandfitness

Read all about football at:
www.ducksters.com/sports/football.php

For all the latest NFL information, check out:
www.nflrush.com

Sports Illustrated online has all the latest football news at:
www.sikids.com

Publisher's note to educators and parents: Our editors have carefully reviewed these websites to ensure that they are suitable for students. Many websites change frequently, however, and we cannot guarantee that a site's future contents will continue to meet our high standards of quality and educational value. Be advised that students should be closely supervised whenever they access the Internet.

INDEX